TRANSFORMED

FROM ABUSED & ADDICTED
TO LIVING A LIFE OF PURPOSE & LOVE

DALLAS FREEMAN

TRANSFORMED
FROM ABUSED & ADDICTED TO LIVING A LIFE OF PURPOSE & LOVE
By Dallas Freeman

Published by:

 LIFEWISE BOOKS

PO BOX 1072
Pinehurst, TX 77362
LifeWiseBooks.com

Interior Layout and Design | Yvonne Parks | PearCreative.ca

To Contact the Author:
www.dallasfreeman.com

ISBN (Print): 978-1-947279-09-4
ISBN (Ebook): 978-1-947279-08-7

DEDICATION

I would like to dedicate this book to everyone who helped me get to this place in my life. I am who I am today first because of God, and secondly because of all of you who have taken the time to love, support, guide, and be there for me while I navigated my healing and transformation.

Words can't express how grateful I am for each of you.

From the bottom of my heart, thank you!

ACKNOWLEDGEMENTS

Thank you to LifeWise Books and Launch Author Coaching for walking me through this process.

Thank you to everyone that encouraged me to write this book and tell my story. Thank you to everyone that invested financial into this project.

You helped make me dream become a reality.

TABLE OF CONTENTS

INTRODUCTION

When I think back over my life, I think and about how extremely blessed I am to be where I am today. I have amazing friends who have become family and I have hope. As a kid, I didn't know where I would end up in life. I'm not sure that I really thought about it outside of the normal kid dreams. I wanted to be a police officer. I wanted to be a lawyer. I was going to own a McDonald's. That's as far as my thoughts went and usually they didn't last very long. For me, life was about surviving through another day of hell. See, I grew up in an environment where drugs and alcohol were like bread and milk. They were very normal for my family.

I have lived a life filled with abuse, addiction and rejection.

I was bullied. I tried to cope in any way I could, which led to my own addiction, sexual promiscuity, and an abortion. My childhood was infused with pain, disappointment, and depression. When I was 22 I came to a place where I wanted to die. I couldn't handle my reality anymore. It was then that I learned who God was and what it meant to have a relationship with Him. It was life changing for me. It was in this moment that things began to turn around. I started the process of healing emotionally, and created a life filled with hope and joy. I was able to overcome a childhood filled with despair and help others do the same.

I want to share a little bit of my journey with you. My hope is that you will be encouraged. As we go on this adventure together, I hope you will learn that all things are possible. I want you to see that abuse and addiction doesn't have to continue to affect your life. It is possible to move past it. I want you to see that we don't have to be defined by our circumstances. You can change your family tree. Your story may be different than mine. Abuse may not have caused your pain. It may be something else that has greatly affected you. I pray you see that there is life beyond your pain. You don't have to stay hurt and wounded. You will come out on the other side, if you choose to. You can be victorious.

CHAPTER 1

DAMAGED

Violated

I was around 4 years old when I was first exposed to inappropriate sexual behavior. I had a family member that masturbated in front of me on a regular basis. While I only remember vague details about these ongoing events, it was just the beginning of the sexual abuse I would endure in my life. I didn't know it then, but the abuses would go on for twelve more years.

Another family member would watch me take showers and come in the room while I was sleeping and touch me inappropriately. This starting happening to me when I was about nine years old. It started with the inappropriate touching. I didn't understand what was going on. This was something I had not experienced before. I had questions. *What was my body doing? Why couldn't I control it? Was it okay that this was happening?*

I knew that what was happening felt good physically and I enjoyed that feeling. However, emotionally it felt wrong. I was embarrassed that I was being touched and that I couldn't control how my body reacted to the touching. I was ashamed that somehow my little conscience knew this behavior was wrong and didn't make me feel good emotionally, but a part of me didn't want to always stop it right away. I would be awakened by someone playing down in my vaginal area. Once I woke up I would start tossing and turning so my abuser would realize I was awake and leave the room.

This happened on and off by the same abuser until I was 16. Each time it would take me a while to come forward and say something to an adult. Once I did it would stop, but only for a while. My abuser would also watch me take showers as I got older. They would sit in the bathroom, open the shower door, look at me, and talk to me while I was showering. This was always extremely uncomfortable. Eventually, I tried to avoid taking showers if they were around.

The older I got the more I despised what was happening. I realized the affects the sexual abuse was having on me. The more I realized, the more I didn't want to deal with it. My answer was to bury myself in school, work, and anything else that would keep me unavailable. In fact, I tried to just not be around at all. I started working whenever I could. I used to go wash dishes, and once I turned twelve, I would babysit just about every weekend so I could avoid my abuser as much as possible.

I figured the less I was around, the less my body was accessible, and the less someone would use it for their pleasure.

This decade of abuse instilled in me an extremely twisted view of sex. What I thought about sex, and what I thought about myself was not at all normal. The sexual abuse I endured set the stage for years of confusion and struggles with sexual sin.

Battered

I was a good kid for the most part, but I remember I felt like I couldn't do anything right. I often felt like people despised my existence. I came home many times to my family tweaked out or drunk and angry. Then the fighting would begin. It never ended well. Sexual abuse was not the only abuse I dealt with. I was also physically abused. This didn't start until I was about twelve. Every time I was slammed against a wall or hit I would become more and more hardened emotionally. The abuse caused me to become a person who lived on the defense. I began to expect the physical abuse and wanted to make sure I was mentally prepared for whatever might come my way.

I remember one day we had family friends over and the other kids and I wanted to get away from the adults for a bit. I had asked for permission to go for a walk. I was immediately told we couldn't go for a walk. I said, "Okay."

My family member stepped toward me and I took a step back. Now, I didn't ask again, but I was told no again. So, I said, "Okay," again.

They stepped closer and again, I stepped back. I was told no another time. I responded again with, "Okay."

After I was told I couldn't go again and I again responded, "Okay," I backed up against the wall. I was told one last time I couldn't go for a walk, but this time I said "Okay. I'm not going for a walk. You don't have to keep telling me no."

I was slapped hard three times across the face. Slapped in front of my friends. I was humiliated. I couldn't believe what just happened was in front of other people, especially my peers. This was the first time something like this had happened with other people around to see it. It wouldn't be the last. I was slammed up against the walls more times than I can remember. I was hit and had things thrown at me. A pattern of abuse developed in my house and it continued until I moved out. At only seventeen, I felt like I didn't matter. To my family, I was nothing more than a punching bag.

Never Good Enough

Looking back, outside of the sexual abuse, the emotional abuse and rejection have had the greatest effect on my life long term. I won't pretend to remember all the mean things that were said to me, but I do know that there were plenty. I grew up being compared to other people. I was often asked why I wasn't as good as this person or that person. Why didn't I do as well as so and so? I always did my best, and I never had an answer. It seemed I just couldn't compete with other people.

By this time, I had developed a smart mouth and used it as a defense mechanism during altercations. My mouth usually landed me in hot water. However, I was doomed before my words were even spoken. I would come home to find my family intoxicated. A fight often ensued, usually over nothing. I took the trash out, I didn't take the trash out...you name it, and there was likely a fight about it at some point. The fights quickly escalated into yelling and arguing. These scenarios also played out in front of other people, which only added to my embarrassment.

These patterned behaviors started happening in middle school and led to multiple times I was told to leave my house and not come back. In the eighth grade, I was told to leave and they truly meant it. What could I do? I got on my bicycle, with only the clothes on my back, and went to a friend's house. I asked if I could please stay the night. I stayed there for three weeks before I went home.

I would have stayed longer but my family made me come home. They had company coming into town and didn't want the company to know I wasn't living there. They told me if I didn't come home they would call the police and have them bring me home. This was the first time I left for such a long time, but it wasn't the last. Leaving became a consistent pattern until I was seventeen. I never knew when I would be kicked out again or how long I would be gone before they made me return home. Dealing with the verbal abuse and the rejection I felt each time I was told to leave caused me to feel defeated and worthless. I wondered why I was even born.

I was never allowed to take anything with me when I was sent away. So, after breaking into the house a few times when no one was there, I finally just kept a bag of clothes and toiletries stashed at a couple different friend's houses. Eventually, I kept a uniform in my locker at work. (I learned that one after I almost got fired for showing up to work without my uniform.) Praise God, I never had to spend a night on the street. Someone always took me in.

This cycle of verbal abuse, emotional abuse, and escape became the way I learned to function; without security in my living situation. So many times I thought, *"Will this be the night I'm told to get out? If it is, which friend will be best to call this time?"* I often thought about whether or not there would ever be a day when things would be different. Eventually I lost hope that things would ever change.

I think this is why I fight so hard for stability in living situations now. If my world is in chaos, but my housing situation is stable, I am always okay. If my home is not secure, I start to panic and freak out a little.

CHAPTER 2

BEER, VODKA, AND DRUGS

Alcohol was the Way of Life

I grew up in a place where drinking was the way of life. It was a Spring Break destination for college students. The vacationers drank and so did most of the locals. Drinking and getting drunk was normal to me. I spent many childhood days hanging out in pubs and outdoor bars. There was a part of that scene that was great to a little kid. I had all the chicken wings, burgers, and fries a kid could ever want. The outdoor bars provided endless pool time, shuffle board, and sandcastles. The pubs provided video games and billiard tables. Not to mention, I had lots of adults to help keep me entertained. It wasn't until I was in the double digits that I started to suspect the environment was not a good one for my family or me. Eventually I learned I was right.

Things in my house remained pretty calm when beer was the only alcohol that people drank. Beer didn't cause many issues. However, the beer drinking led to vodka drinking. The problems began with vodka. I knew anything could happen when vodka was around. When I saw the vodka being consumed, my insecurity, worry, and fear would begin to well up inside me. It was in these moments when fights would ensue, manipulation happened, and hurtful things were said. Vodka was the vice that caused the lashing out and the anger that resulted in physical and emotional abuse.

I remember one time I had a couple of my friend's over. I didn't have friends over often, but these girls knew about my environment and came over every once in a while. While they were over the adults began to drink vodka. A fight broke out and I was thrown out. They had to stand there and watch me as I was told to leave my house. They had to stand there while I was physically thrown out and forbidden to take anything with me. I was absolutely mortified and ashamed. It was one thing for me to be rejected and abandoned in secret. It was another thing for other people to see the rejection and abandonment happen.

How was I supposed to look at my friends after they saw this?

How could other people possibly love or value you when they watched you being thrown out like the trash? How do you recover from that? Each time I was thrown out or verbally abused another piece of my dignity and self-worth ripped away. Eventually I had none. I didn't understand why my life was like this.

Pizza, Cocaine, and the DEA

When I was twelve, my family and I found jobs working at a pizza restaurant for a close family friend. I was hired to do dishes and paid under the table. Thus began my official working life. My family also took jobs at the restaurant delivering pizzas. It wasn't long before I discovered the owner was a drug dealer and my family was doing drugs. He was notorious and he controlled the cocaine market on Fort Myers Beach. He would later be responsible for a few murders and several other crimes, and he was my family's drug dealer.

He began coming to the house and when he did he gave me fifty dollars and sent me to the arcade to play games. This was back when video games were twenty-five and fifty cents, so the money he gave me kept me away for quite a while. One time I showed up for work at the restaurant a little early. I saw stacks and stacks of money and cocaine. I was scared. I didn't know what to think. I was reprimanded for showing up early. I'm sure it was because I was never supposed to see the money or cocaine. From that moment on I was always a little uneasy at work.

Sometime later, I went to the bus stop in front of the pizza place. There were DEA agents everywhere! I knew this was not good and people were going to jail, maybe even my family. For a second I thought maybe I would be taken in for working illegally under age. Neither my family nor I went to jail that day, but after that I went back to babysitting. I never saw drugs in my house again. I think my family stopped using cocaine because they didn't have a supply source or the extra job to pay for it. That was fine by me.

Surviving

I spent my high school years in survival mode. I went to school. I worked, often forty hours a week. I socialized when I could. I decided to survive in my environment until I could change it. I vowed I would not be like my family. I vowed that I would be different. I wanted to make better choices. I was going to make a way for myself and not look back.

It wasn't long after I graduated high school that I began to realize how unhappy I was. After high school, I had more time on my hands. In a way, the idle time forced me to admit how I was really feeling. It forced me to see that I was unhappy and extremely hurt. I didn't know how to process these feelings.

My way of processing eventually involved drugs and alcohol. Two of the very things I tried to avoid my whole childhood. I started out smoking pot. Smoking pot allowed me to escape my reality. It relaxed me and I felt like it cleared my head. I enjoyed the escape it gave me recreationally (which was often).

I got drunk for the first time on my 21st birthday. I ended up stripping on my coffee table in front of a room full of people. It was not one of my finest moments for sure. I went on to have many more drunken nights. I never liked the taste of alcohol but I enjoyed the care free joyful spirit it gave me. Since I didn't like the taste I would do shots. I partied like this a lot. I was responsible, so I thought. I went to work every day. I paid my bills. I never drank and drove. I kept chasing that good feeling. I survived my days and wasted my nights partying it up and escaping my feelings.

My friends started doing ecstasy during this time. They didn't tell me because they thought I would be upset with them. Believe or not, I was considered the "goody-goody" of the group. Once they told me about how ecstasy made them feel I decided I wanted to try it. I wanted everything I touched to feel good. I wanted to love everyone and everything without a care in the world. I tried it. It became my drug of choice. I took ecstasy every weekend and any night I was off work the next day. It provided the ultimate escape for me. I thought it helped me to just love life and love people. I look back at this now and wonder what I was thinking. This stuff had heroine in it and who knows what else.

There are a lot of things about this time in my life that I am not proud of. I became someone who drank and did drugs. I became responsible for other people doing drugs because I convinced them to try the drugs. I provided a place for people to party. I helped my friends pay for their drugs. I became a person who lived my life trying to escape my life. I had become the very person I strived my whole life to not be. I was on a downward spiral and didn't even realize it.

CHAPTER 3

GLIMPSES OF NORMAL

Chocolate Milk

My life wasn't all bad. There were some great times. When I was in kindergarten my mom would drive me to school. There were many mornings we would stop at the store on the way and pick up a chocolate milk. At that time, single serve chocolate milks still came in the cardboard containers. My mom was always worried I would spill it in the car. To prevent me from riding in the car with a full on open container of chocolate milk the lady at the convenient store would always cut a hole in the top of the carton and put a straw in it. So, basically, I had my own custom-made juice box. I still love chocolate milk to this day.

Nana

My Nana (grandmother) was one of my favorite people on the planet when I was growing up. I lived with her until I was seven. I never moved more than five miles away from her. I loved going to her house. Nana used to come home from work and change into her house dress right away. When she did she would sit with her feet on the floor and her legs a little open. This created the perfect little seat for me in her dress. There were days I couldn't wait until she got home so I could sit in her dress and hear about her day.

Nana was creative and enjoyed her crafts. I have two quilts that she made me when I was little. One of them has some of my baby clothes quilted into it. The other quilt is filled with childhood memories. She covered it with things that I liked, things that she liked, and special things like the pockets from my cousins' jackets. The tradition was that I would sleep with the quilt every holiday's eve. Then when I woke up any pocket, zipper, or empty place would be stuffed with a prize inside.

Christmas was her favorite holiday. She started preparing for Christmas in January. She saved her change all year so she was sure I would have a Christmas present. On Christmas morning, we would all open our gifts and then the grab box would circulate. The grab box was a huge box filled with presents marked girl, boy, or neutral. We would take turns grabbing presents until it was empty. The grab box contained things you needed but made boring gifts. Batteries, socks, and underwear were just a few of the items you might get.

My Nana was truly a breath of fresh air in a life that was full of turmoil. I miss her very much.

Kindness

I was always blessed to have people in my life that loved me. I look back and see so many people that God placed in my life to help me get through the hard times. People who accepted me just as I was. People that weren't scared away by my home life. People that wanted to provide me some sense of normalcy and safety.

Dee was a woman who was older than me. In fact, she used to babysit me when I was little. When I was old enough, I babysat her son Mikey. They became family to me. Mikey still tells people I am his sister and I tell people he is my brother. I've known him since he was a baby. They included me in everything they did. I spent a lot of my free time with them at their house. They took me in numerous times when I needed a place to stay. I always knew I had a place with them and never felt like a burden.

I didn't have many friends my age, but the ones I did have were top notch. In middle school, I found a few girls who became great friends to me. They were my best friends by high school. These girls probably do not realize how important they were for me. Spending time with them provided a place of refuge from the craziness that was happening at home. The sleepovers, parties, weekly skate nights, and hanging out provided places to escape and just be a kid. They also provided support, encouragement, understanding and shoulders to cry on when needed. As a teenager going through hell, they were lifesavers.

I worked with another lady when I was fourteen, who became very important to me. Her name was Momma V. She waitressed at a restaurant where I bussed tables while going to college. She never thought of me as some kid that she had to work with. She always took time to talk to me. She always listened to me and genuinely cared about what I was saying. Momma V. invited me over to the house to spend time with her family. She told me how special I was and told me regularly that things would get better. Things would get easier. She was and is someone very near and dear to my heart.

Difference Makers

School was a place where I knew that for at least seven hours a day I didn't have to deal with my home life. While the kids at school weren't always very nice to me, the teachers and staff were. I had several teachers and school staff who went above and beyond to invest in my life and made me feel safe, loved, and wanted. My elementary school principal was one of those people. She kept up with me all the way through my high school graduation. She called to check in on me, and I went by to see her when I could. She always had a smile for me and offered words of encouragement. She always told me I could do anything I put my mind to.

The bookkeeper at my high school and my high school principal were also vital to my success there. One of my classes required us to perform community service hours, so I helped the bookkeeper. We developed a good relationship. I told her about the abuse I had been dealing with at home. I explained that the abuse was why social workers were coming to school to check on me. She would talk with me and let me vent. Some days I just wanted to quit because school, work, and life was too much. She would encourage me to keep fighting for my victory and remind me that my circumstances were only temporary.

My high school principal never let me take the easy route. She knew I had not experienced an easy life. She also knew I had the potential to make something of myself. She loved me, showed me grace, and supported me. She saw something in me and would never let me give less than my best. She also pushed me to be better than I thought I could be. She gave me tough love when I needed it. She never accepted mediocrity from me. She didn't let me throw in the towel or give excuses.

I don't know if there are words to express what these three ladies mean to me and how they have impacted my life. These ladies gave extra of themselves to me when they didn't have to, in order to ensure I graduated and didn't get lost in the shuffle. I can only hope that even though I went down the wrong path for a bit, they look at my life now, are proud that I turned things around. I made a good life for myself. I hope they understand that their investment in my life helped to shape who I am and taught me how to invest in others.

CHAPTER 4

BORN LOSER

Ogre

School was a safe place for me for such a long time. It was a place I enjoyed going to because it got me away from my reality. I was not the popular kid by any means. I didn't have time to worry about wearing make-up or doing my hair a certain way. I was pretty much a tomboy. I never really excelled at sports. I was teased a lot. The teasing crossed over to bullying in middle and high school. Once the bullying got bad I didn't have that escape anymore. They stole my safety. They brought pain into my happy place.

I remember a time I was riding my bike over by the elementary school when a group of girls spotted me. They came over and surrounded me. They started saying mean things to me and calling me names. The girls threatened to beat me up and I just knew they were going to do it. I managed to escape the situation but it was scary. Before the girls were able to get a swing in, I punched one of them in the arm. When I did, her arm flew back and hit another girl in the face. That distraction allowed me to escape. They chased me but couldn't catch up. I was grateful I came out of the situation unharmed physically.

There was a period of time in middle school, when the kids on the bus would chant, "Ogre! Ogre!" It happened both to and from school. They were relentless. It got to the point I didn't want to go to school anymore because the bus was the only way I could get there. This continual bullying almost brought me to a breaking point. I felt so dejected. I didn't want the kids to see me hurt so I would never cry. I figured that if I cried it would only make things worse.

An incident in ninth grade brought mixed emotions. It was homecoming time. Everyone was casting their votes for homecoming king and queen for their grade. When the announcement was made I was shocked to hear my name called as Homecoming Queen for the freshman class. I couldn't believe I was voted in! Maybe I was popular? Maybe more people liked me than I thought? After all, I was just made

Homecoming Queen and the quarterback of the J.V. football team was King. How cool was this?

My excitement turned to devastation. I found out quickly from some of the kids at school that they had nominated me and voted me in as a big joke. For some reason, a group of my peers thought it would be funny. Now I had to go to the game and be presented to the school and community as Homecoming Queen! I had to walk the field with the King. The next night I went to the dance (as required) and had to dance with the King, all while I knew it was a horrible joke.

The whole situation had me mortified, and left feeling humiliated. I didn't even want to walk down the hallways. I knew everyone was talking about me. They were either laughing at me or feeling sorry for me. I didn't want them to do either. I just wanted them to get to know me, be nice to me, or at least just leave me alone. I wouldn't have wished this experience on anyone. My spirit took a crushing blow by the whole thing and I never thought I would recover.

Breaking Down

I didn't think I had any kind of a future. My life consisted of surviving each day. Eventually I lost hope that things would ever be better. All I saw were my current circumstances. I never felt good enough for anyone or anything. I often wondered if somebody would even notice if I wasn't around. What if I just packed up and left? If I just took off and started a new life somewhere else, would people care? These were the thoughts that often went through my mind. I couldn't understand why my life was like this. What did I do to deserve it? What could I do to stop it all?

The abuse and the bullying stripped me of any value I had. I truly believed I was not worth anything. In my mind, the two reasons I was around were for people to use as a punching bag (literally and figuratively), or to be used for their sexual pleasure. I couldn't understand how people who were supposed to love and protect me caused me such anguish.

The words that had been spoken to me and the actions I endured left me feeling insignificant and unwanted. It got so bad that eventually I expected the worst in every situation and lived my life on the defense. The people causing the devastation in my life were never going to know that they slowly broke me down. I put up a front. As far as they were concerned I was "just fine," and I could handle anything they threw at me. I became so good at putting up the front, that even I couldn't see how far it was from the truth. I was literally dying inside.

Needing My Tribe

I didn't believe I belonged anywhere even though I had a tremendous desire to fit, to have my own tribe. I came to the conclusion that my family didn't want me. If they did, I would have been treated differently. If I wasn't a part of my own family then where was my place? I often felt like a burden to the people who helped me during my childhood. They never said or acted like I was a problem, I just assumed I was and felt bad for it. After all, I was another mouth to feed. I required a shower and a place to sleep. I desired attention and love. All these resources were valuable. I didn't want to take them from the people they belonged to, even if they offered them. I wasn't worthy. I wasn't their responsibility. They didn't choose me.

I tried to make sure I did whatever I could to earn people's love so they would include me and want me around. I behaved and helped around the house. I bought gifts and attempted to take care of the people who took care of me. I always tried to pay my own way. I knew that if they abandoned me I was in real trouble. I literally had nowhere else to go. This scared me and I didn't know how to process the fact that I was completely reliant on the generosity of people who were not my family.

I didn't have a relationship with God at this time in my life, but there were nights I was curled up in a ball and begged God to make everything go away. I pleaded with him to give me the strength to make it one more day. I didn't understand why I wanted to make it another day, but I did. Every time I was pushed to the point of a breakdown and asked God for help, I felt a strength rise up in me to fight one more time. He was with me during those days even though I didn't fully realize it.

CHAPTER 5

LOOKING FOR LOVE IN ALL THE WRONG PLACES

Anybody and Everybody

When I was nineteen I moved to Texas. I thought maybe if I just got away from Florida I would be happy. While there, I quickly made a friend. We used to go out and do all sorts of things. Unfortunately, one of them was sleeping with any guy that had something nice to say to me. When a guy gave me a compliment, even if it was for just for a minute, I felt good about myself. I would immediately sleep with him. It didn't matter where we were. One time we were in a car in the parking lot. I figured sex was what he wanted. I thought it was my job to provide him with that pleasure, so I did.

I went to Mardi Gras in Galveston that year. It was a fun time and I met a lot of people. My friend and I met some guys and brought them back to our hotel room. We ended up taking turns having threesomes with the guys. Physically, the sex gave me pleasure. Emotionally I was void. There was no love or attraction with these guys or any of the others. I was just doing my duty.

It wasn't just random guys that I had sex with. Eventually, I ended up having sex with a lot of my guy friends as well. I'd be hanging out and partying with my friends and somehow something would start and one thing would lead to another and it would end in sex. I cared about my friends. I wanted them to be happy and taken care of. This was a way I thought I could help. It was a tool I could use to earn acceptance and approval. Who better to gain acceptance and approval from than your friends.

There was a time when I was struggling to pay my rent money. I confided in a guy friend of mine that I wasn't sure what I was going to do. I had no idea how I would get the money in time. I was very stressed out. He offered to give me the money. This was such a relief. I quickly found out there was a string attached. If I wanted the money all I had to do was perform oral sex for him. I couldn't believe it. He was just another person who wanted something from me. I was desperate though, so I did it. I was humiliated. I felt degraded.

Did I really just perform sexual favors for rent money? What was happening to me? Who was I becoming? I know now that it was the sexual abuse that left me feeling like my body was for the taking, to be used for others and their needs. I actually thought sex was something I was supposed to offer to people. Sex was not something I viewed as an intimate act that was meant for the sanctity of marriage. There was nothing special or sacred about it. It was this dirty and shameful thing in my mind. My body was not worth saving for someone special because no one special was going to want me.

Those were the real thoughts in my head and I didn't have the answers. This situation just reaffirmed to me that I was good for one thing only and that was to be a sex toy. I didn't realize it but I was sinking further and further into a pit of despair and destruction.

Desperate for Affection

I was conflicted. I thought sex was this awful thing, but I also longed for true affection. I didn't want this kind of affection from men. I wanted it from women. I had a void in my heart for motherly acceptance and I began to seek it out. My desire for this affection soon twisted and I became attracted to women. I had my first sexual experience with a woman when I was nineteen. It was my friend from Texas. The more I got to know her the more I wanted to know her and desired her closeness. This was new territory for my young mind and I didn't know how to process it all. We became really good friends.

One night she told me she had feelings for me that were more than friendship. We talked about her feelings and I began to share my desire for female affection with her. This was my first, but would not be my only female sexual relationship. I went on to date other women, while still sleeping with men. The women had the emotional connection that had been missing and I was comfortable with girls. I didn't feel like a play toy.

These relationships weren't random for me. During this time of my life, they were meaningful, intimate, and beautiful. I never went out to find and meet a girl to date. It was always someone I was friends with first. Then the desperation for affection, mixed with the attraction would increase until I felt sex was inevitable. I wasn't gay or bisexual, even though I was acting that way. I was a confused young girl searching for some sort of healing and wholeness. Therefore, I participated in anything that might provide that for me.

The years of sexual abuse skewed my perception of sex, intimacy, and healthy relationships of any kind. I dreamed of a husband, kids, and a house with a white picket fence. I wasn't sure it would ever happen for me but it was what I wanted. I didn't know what my dream really looked like because I had never seen it. So, instead I looked to others to fill my voids and take my pain away. I soon realized that no person was ever going to be able to do that for me and it wasn't fair for me to expect them to.

Hitting Bottom

One night I went out with a guy from work. We had become pretty good work friends and had hung out a few times. On this particular night we were going on a date. The date ended up being a one night stand. We had a lot of fun and ended up back at my house having sex. It wasn't long after this that I started feeling sick. Constantly throwing up and tired all the time. Someone mentioned that they thought I might be pregnant. I thought, "There's no way." Eventually, I decided to take a pregnancy test and it was positive.

What was I going to do now? At first I was shocked and a little freaked out. My next emotion was excitement. I was going to have a baby! A child of my very own. A human that was going to love me no matter what. Then I started wondering how I would ever take care of a baby. I was a huge mess myself and was in no position to raise a little human. What was I thinking?

I told the dad what was going on and he wanted no part of it. He had no intention in helping me raise or support the baby.

He told me to get an abortion and that if I didn't I should expect nothing from him. Ever. My response was, "No way!"

I didn't believe in abortion. My mindset was always that if you were old enough to have sex you were old enough to handle the responsibilities that came with sex. This was a human life we were talking about. I couldn't just kill a human life. I honestly didn't know what I was going to do.

Time passed and the more I thought about what kind of world I would be bringing the baby into with me as a mom and no dad. I went against what I believed and eventually made the decision to have an abortion. I decided the baby was better off not being born. I didn't think that the baby had a fighting chance in the real world. I went to the abortion clinic scared and confused.

I don't remember much about that day or the experience. I know I went in pregnant and came out not pregnant. I left the clinic feeling dirty, ashamed, guilty, and so very sad. I just wanted to take a shower and forget the whole thing ever happened. I killed a human. A human that was growing inside me. The baby was part me and was unable to fight for itself. I was forced to deal with the consequences of my decisions. I couldn't look at myself in the mirror for days and wondered if I would ever recover. All seemed hopeless.

CHAPTER 6

DESPERATE FOR CHANGE

Infected and Injured

The abortion was the final straw. It took me on a downward spiral to rock bottom fast. I literally hated myself. Like I said, I truly couldn't look at myself in the mirror, but when I did all I saw was guilt, disgust, and shame. For two months, I went to work and did ecstasy. That was my existence. I decided that things were always going to be the way they currently were. I was never going to know true happiness and what that felt like. I honestly didn't think I deserved it.

I was destined to a life of misery and I couldn't understand why. I had been told that God was a loving God. If that was true, then why had all these things happened to me? I was convinced that God didn't love me either. I assumed he had left me and I was truly alone.

Survival mode was in full effect and I had to fight to get through each minute of every day. In these moments, I felt I had been deceived by life. For some reason I always believed that if I tried and fought hard enough I could rise above everything that was thrown at me. I was a fighter and not a quitter. I didn't have to be the victim of my circumstances. I decided that none of this was true. I was never going to rise above. I was always going to be a victim. I could not see a way out of my current circumstances or hurts.

I didn't know how to make the pain go away, but I knew I didn't want to keep feeling it. I tried so hard to make the pain go away. I drank, did drugs, slept around, got piercings, shaved my head, worked a lot, and took care of others. None of this was effective. It was like trying to put a bandaid on a wound that needed staples and stitches. It was all temporary and didn't provide healing to my infected and injured heart.

I was depressed and desperate for a different reality. I often thought about cutting myself. I figured the physical pain would take away the emotional pain or at least serve as a distraction. I'm not sure why I never did. I credit it to God protecting me from yet another thing I would have had to overcome in the future.

Ending It All

Suicide was very real to me. My best friend tried to commit suicide. I will never forget how terrified I was when she told me how many pills she swallowed. I will never forget the feeling of helpless fear I felt as I sat there at the hospital while they pumped her stomach. Time stopped. I remember having to make the phone call to her mom and ask her to make the six-hour trip up as soon as she could, because I wasn't sure if her daughter was going to make it.

It was a few days before we knew that she was going to live, and that with a little help she would never try to kill herself again. Those were the longest days of my life. I felt so helpless. The relief I experienced when I learned my friend was going to live and not die is unexplainable. She got the help she needed and found true joy and happiness. I no longer had to worry.

About two months after my abortion, I just wanted it all to stop. I couldn't handle life in its current state anymore. I didn't want to die but I didn't want to live another day either. I was miserable but there was something deep down in me that still had a desire to live. It was more than not wanting anyone else to experience the feeling I felt when I thought my friend was going to die. Death scared me. I wasn't ready to leave the world, yet I knew there had to be change or I wouldn't survive. Allowing things to continue as they were was not an option. I was confident that without change, suicide would be my future.

I was desperate for the pain to go away. I knew I needed to dream again but I had real questions that needed answers. *What do I do? How do I fix this? What have I not tried?* I needed to figure out what other options existed out there. It wasn't long after these thoughts and questions filled my mind that my life would change forever. It took one decision.

CHAPTER 7

FOREVER CHANGED

Nothing to Wear

I will never forget the day that Jesus came into my life. I was a 22-year-old girl with no hope, no love, and no self-worth. I had exhausted all avenues in an attempt to find happiness and all had ended with regret and reinforced my feelings of inadequacy.

One day my best friend and I got into a stupid fight over something I can't even remember. The argument brought me to a place of complete despair. In that moment, I realized my life had completely unraveled and I was hanging on by a thread. I was in so much pain and I had lost so much. I couldn't bear the thought of losing another person and I was so terrified she was going to end our friendship. I didn't feel like I would be able to handle one more ounce of pain or rejection.

It was in this moment that I broke. I mean, I couldn't get the flood of tears to stop. I told her that I didn't want to kill myself but I didn't know what else to do because I couldn't handle any more of this life. She suggested that we go to church. Her mom had been trying to get us to go for two years. I started to say no, because I thought she was crazy for even suggesting such a thing. In my mind, there was no way I could go to church because of how I looked and felt. I had a shaved head, eyebrow ring, tongue ring, no "church" clothes, only big, baggy jeans and clubbing clothes. I feared they wouldn't even let me in the door. Even if they did, I wasn't sure what would happen. *Would the church fall down? Would everyone stare? Would I be allowed to stay?*

I eventually gave in and agreed to go to a youth service. To my surprise no one stopped me at the door and refused to let me in. I walked into the youth room which was in a gym. There were video games and moving lights. There was fun music playing and all different kinds of people there; teenagers, college age kids, and adults. Everyone was hanging out and having fun talking and playing games. The environment was inviting.

I was welcomed and loved just the way I was. They spent time with me, and they prayed with me. They listened as I shared my story about where I came from and what I was trying to overcome. I had never been around a group of people who didn't want something from me, or didn't need me to take care of them.

Acceptance was new for me. Every person I met at the church embraced me and accepted me. They helped me to begin to learn how to navigate a relationship with God and answered my questions with no judgement. This group was Jesus with skin on. Sometimes it scared me and I didn't always know how to react. I often wondered if it was going to end one day. I am happy to say that I am still friends with all those people and they helped shaped me into the woman I am today.

Meeting My New Best Friend

It was your typical youth service and I enjoyed being there. The service started with worship music. The music was upbeat at first and people were dancing a little and clapping. Then the music slowed down and people were closing their eyes and lifting their hands. I didn't fully understand what was happening but I enjoyed the atmosphere. After the music, they introduced a guest speaker who walked onto the stage and shared a message.

After the message was finished there was an altar call. It's when the speaker asks specific people to come to the front for some particular reason. This time the speaker said that he knew there was a girl in the audience that had been sexually, physically, and emotionally abused. That she was hurt and felt rejected, useless and hopeless; like no one wanted her and her life was a waste. She had tried everything she could think of to be happy and has not succeeded. He said that 'God wants her to know that he loves her and has a plan for her life. He is waiting on her.'

I was so completely shocked that this man knew all this stuff about me. It was like he read my mind. I went up to the front of the room for prayer. I didn't make the decision that night. I wanted to be confident in my decision. All of this gave me a lot to think about.

I spent the next few weeks really searching my soul. See, I had been to church several times before. Anytime I stayed at a friend's house who went to church I went to church right along with them. I just never understood what a relationship with God could do for me. I finally decided it was time to find out. A few weeks later, I gave my life to God. It has absolutely been the best decision I have made in my entire life.

Never the Same

Meeting Jesus, creating and working on a relationship with Him, was exactly what I needed. Once I gave my life to God He radically changed me. I became a completely different person.

I never touched drugs or alcohol again. Soon, my desire for homosexual behavior ceased and I stopped giving my body to whoever wanted it. I began (and have been) saving myself for my husband. I am not going to say that this all happened instantly. It didn't. It was a process. However, every step I took brought me more freedom. The process was worth the result.

I remember one day looking at my life and realizing how much destruction the devil had brought to me. He tried to destroy me and almost succeeded. The grace of God was at work in my life and I never even knew it. As bad as things were, they could have been so much worse. I began to be happy.

God placed my life on a new path, gave me happiness, joy, peace, patience, understanding, and forgiveness. He took the girl I was, the girl with no hope or future, and spoke life into me. I am forever grateful for having met Jesus and allowing Him to take control of my life. I don't know where I would be today without His grace. I can only imagine it wouldn't be anywhere I would want to be today.

CHAPTER 8

THIS THING CALLED LOVE

What is Love?

Love was not a word I understood in a healthy context. I believed it was dependent upon how you acted, what you did for people, and whether or not you pleased them sexually. I did not know Godly, unconditional, biblical love. The Bible says:

> "Love is patient, love is kind. It does not envy, it does not boast, it is not proud. It does not dishonor others, it is not self-seeking, it is not easily angered, it keeps no record of wrongs. Love does not delight in evil but rejoices with the truth. It always protects,

always trusts, always hopes, always perseveres,"
(1 Corinthians 13:4-7 NIV).

Reading this verse from the Bible was like reading a foreign language I did not know. It was the exact opposite of what I believed love was. I had been hurt so much I wasn't fully convinced God would be any different than those who had hurt me. I thought he would bail on me the minute I messed up. My attention was drawn to a verse in the Psalms:

> "For great is your love toward me; you have
> delivered me from the depths, from the realm
> of the dead," (Psalm 86:13 NIV).

This verse spoke straight to my heart. I related to it because it was what happened to me. I was literally delivered from depths of hell. My life had hit bottom and there was nothing left worth living for. In that moment God reached down into that pit and pulled me out. He rescued me from despair. He changed the course of my life.

Learning to love and value myself was not an easy journey. I began the process of renewing my mind and worked hard to grasp the true concept of love. I taped Psalm 139:13-16 on my bathroom mirror and read it every day. It reads:

> "For you created my inmost being; you knit
> me together in my mother's womb. I praise

you because I am fearfully and wonderfully made; your works are wonderful, I know that full well. My frame was not hidden from you when I was made in the secret place, when I was woven together in the depths of the earth. Your eyes saw my unformed body; all the days ordained for me were written in your book before one of them came to be," (NIV).

The more I read this the more I began to believe that I was worth something. If the Creator of the Universe took the time to personally knit me together I must be special. It took a long time before I could say I had a healthy perspective. I continue to learn every day.

Loving God

There is more to know about love. After I learned what the word truly meant I had to grasp that God loved me. I worked on a relationship with the Lord; praying, worshipping, and studying the word. I began to learn His character and to trust Him at His word. He showed me time and time again that He loved me, He was always there for me, and would never leave me. He showed me this in small and big ways.

I remember about three weeks after I met God I decided to go with a group of college kids from my church to tell others about him. I had no idea what I was doing. At this point I didn't even have one scripture memorized, but I wanted to spend time with the kids. We went down to the beach and started talking to people. We met a couple of guys who just wanted to know where they could find the coolest place to party.

My friends started talking to one guy and they were discussing scripture. The other guy was just standing there so I started talking to him. I told him that three weeks ago I was him. I was looking for the party and a good time. Next, I mentioned that I found a party that never ended with Jesus and he should join me at church the next night to see what I was talking about. Saturday night church came and he actually showed up and gave his life to the Lord.

I remember being so surprised at how it all unfolded. God used this event to show me He would always be with me and guiding me. He wouldn't leave me hanging. I just had to listen for His direction. There are hundreds more stories I could share about God coming through for me or showing me his love both directly and through people he has placed in my life. Each of these times helped me to accept his love and to love him a little more.

No Strings Attached

Learning to care about others, and believe they cared about me, was challenging for me. I had to realize that love in its purest form comes without strings attached. It's not based on performance or gifts. I wasn't sure how this was ever going to happen for me. I had accepted and was beginning to understand how God loved me, but would people? It is hard when your heart is involved. Once you have been wounded, your instincts are to protect yourself from perceived danger. For me, people were the perceived danger. Just like you have to learn how to a hold a knife without getting cut, I had to learn how to have relationships even though they could hurt me.

God was very strategic in teaching me. He placed people in my path that were extraordinary. About six months after meeting Jesus I moved to Alabama to participate in an intense nine-month discipleship program. When I first got there, I met a girl by the name of Lindsay. She walked up to me and said, "Hi, are you Dallas?"

With a huge attitude I responded, "Yeah, who are you?"

"I'm Lindsay," she replied very nicely.

We laugh about that story to this day. I was so mean to her and for some reason she kept being nice to me. No matter what I said or did she wouldn't back down. She gave me encouraging notes and cards. She spent time with me. She showered me with love, support, and kindness even when I didn't deserve it and couldn't give it back.

This friendship helped teach me about love. I was not in a place I could do anything for her. I was trying to get my own life in some sort of order. She didn't care. That wasn't on her agenda. Her agenda was to love me and help me through my process. Our friendship has never been about keeping score or how much either of us can take. I have learned a lot from Lindsay and her friendship. The lessons she taught me helped me cultivate many other healthy friendships.

There were many more people placed in my life that have taught me valuable life lessons. It wasn't long after moving to Birmingham that I met Susanne. She was a fireball of a lady. She was extremely passionate about God and still has a zeal for life. She began to meet with me and mentor me. She taught me about faith, tenacity, perseverance, and love. No matter what life threw at her she never gave up.

As our mentoring relationship grew I began to realize that she loved me right where I was. It didn't matter what I did, what I said, or how I acted. Susanne was always there for me. Sometimes I was not sure why because I could be a brat back then, and I had an attitude the size of Texas. She always spoke truth to me. She would always pray with me and gave me comforting hugs. She still does.

Susanne has never stopped telling me how much she believes in me, how proud she is of me, how much potential she knows I have. Time and time again she has demonstrated that love doesn't have to be performed for. It's not something you have to buy. Love is something to be given and received freely. It took me a long time to realize she wasn't going anywhere, and that I couldn't run her off.

Once I realized this, there was freedom for me. I was able to see that I could be myself and people would keep loving and caring. The love wasn't attached to an action, strings, or correct behavior. It was just attached to me. It was in this realization that I began to learn who I really was as a person. I wasn't Dallas the victim of abuse and bad decisions. I was just Dallas.

Each of the people God brought into my life taught me that He was always going to be there for me no matter what. This was a new concept for me but one I am thankful to understand now.

> "But God demonstrates his own love for us in
> this: While we were still sinners, Christ died for
> us," (Romans 5:8 NIV).

He showed his devotion to me through the people he placed in my life, the joy he filled my heart with, and by walking with me day to day. He kept loving me and was by my side even when I didn't know what it meant or that he was there. I can look back at my life and see that God always loved me, even before I knew who he was. He was passionate about me. He protected me when I was making awful decisions. I honestly don't know where I would be without him and I am grateful that he never quit loving me or waiting for me to love him back.

All I Had to Do Was Trust

Trust, much like love, was not an easy process. I had to learn to trust him. I had learned that he loved me, but trust was a whole other thing. All of the hurt and disappointment taught me not to count on other people. I wish I could tell you that I woke up one morning and trusted God, but I didn't. I had to overcome the lie that the only person I could truly rely on was myself.

> "Trust in the Lord with all your heart and lean not on your own understanding; in all your ways submit to him, and he will make your paths straight," (Proverbs 3:5-6 NIV).

This was a lesson that I would gradually learn over time. I started by trying to do the little things I thought he told me to. Every time I did what God told me to, he always provided for me.

He always showed me that he was right there walking with me. Sometimes it was in subtle ways and sometimes in big ways.

There were also times when I didn't know what I was supposed to do or how things were going to work out. God would always remind me that he was with me and he had it handled. He was directing my path. All I had to do was trust. I remember once when God really pressed me to trust Him at a whole new level. It was suggested to me by a few church friends that I go to a discipleship program. The idea excited me, but I wasn't sure I could do something like that. However, I felt a peace inside about taking the steps to at least research a few places where this program existed and maybe even apply to some.

It turned out that three different locations were recommended. I called them all and had them send me information. As soon as I received the information I knew that two of them were out right away. I had no interest whatsoever, but I kept going back to the packet from Birmingham. I was drawn to it. At first, I was a little turned off because of all the rules. The more I thought about it, I began to think that rules might be good for me for a bit. I had been taking care of myself since I was twelve and I had clearly not done that well. So, I decided to fill out the application. When I completed it, I was filled with excitement and knew that if they would take me, this was the place for me.

I just knew God was telling me to go there, but I still thought he was crazy! I was a manager of a restaurant, and I had bills and a life. I didn't have nine months to spend in Alabama! Plus, there was the issue of money. How was I going to pay for the program? I knew the kids who went couldn't work while they were there because of classes and traveling. Tuition was almost $4,000 not including gas, food, cell phone bill, car insurance, and spending money. There was no way I was going to raise that kind of cash in three months. Crazy!

Well, one by one, I took the steps God told me take. I worked. I saved. I got rid of my car with car payments and got a car that was paid in full. All this while waiting to find out if I was even going to be accepted into the program. You can probably imagine, I was eventually accepted and I paid my thousand dollars for the down payment. I continued to do all I knew to do. During the process, I found out that my church in Florida offered the same program, however, it was recommended that I look at programs out of state. I knew it would be better for me to go to a place where I didn't have access all my old vices. If I couldn't run to drugs, alcohol, and sex, I would have to run to God and let Him help me face my pain and fears. I prayed about this in the small way I knew how to pray. I decided leaving Florida would be the best for me.

I moved to Alabama a few short months later and gave them every last penny I had to cover the rest of my tuition. Now what? I had to live there for nine months with no job. What was I thinking? I decided this was not the most responsible thing I had ever done. It would take me another book to tell you all the ways that God provided during this time. I will tell you that I never went without food or anything else I needed and I didn't go without much I wanted either. I stayed in that program for three more years and every year my costs were always covered.

One year a couple I had never met sent four thousand dollars for tuition on my behalf. All these things God did for me taught me that I could trust him in every way.

> "Never will I leave you; never will I forsake you," (Hebrews13:5 NIV).

God showed me that he was not going anywhere every day in the ways he provided for me, protected me, loved me when I was unlovable, knew my deepest pains and regret, and still comforted me. He taught me how to love and how to trust. I am so glad he did because it has filled my life with great joy.

CHAPTER 9

TIME FOR SURGERY

I Believe in You

I knew early on in my walk with God that I had a lot of issues that needed to be dealt with. The only way I was going to overcome my past circumstances and personal choices was to face them head on and allow myself to feel the pain so I could heal emotionally. I wasn't quite sure how to go about doing this or if it was even possible. I was pretty messed up from the years of abuse, and my own bad choices.

This is where going to the discipleship program in Alabama helped me. I had the time and people to help guide and teach me how to develop a relationship with God. I was in an atmosphere that would give me the space and guidance to heal.

I knew that being able to gain a strong foundation for my new life was vital.

Moving to Alabama to be part of this program provided me with more than I could have ever dreamed. I had a safe place to learn how to hear God's voice, time to focus on my emotional well-being, and lifelong friends who have and continue to stand with me through the good and the bad. It was the place where I began to dream of a future.

> "For I know the plans I have for you, declares the Lord, plans to prosper you and not to harm you, plans to give you hope and a future" (Jeremiah 29:11 NIV).

I'll never forget my third day in Alabama. We went on a retreat so we could all get to know each other. The first night of retreat Pastor Sims walked up to me and looked me in the eyes. He said "I believe in you."

My mind began asking questions. *Who was he talking to? It couldn't be me. Why would anyone say that to me? I am a mess. There is nothing to believe in here.* I tried desperately to avoid eye contact with him. Maybe I felt if I couldn't see his eyes then I didn't have to hear what he was saying. He said it to me three or four more times. The last time he grabbed my face so I couldn't look away and he again said "I believe in you."

When it finally sunk in that he was talking to me, something shifted inside. I had never heard those words before. Now that someone believed in me, I wanted to fight harder to overcome my adversities. It gave me a sense of pride. Someone cared about me, believed in who I was as a person, and who I could become even though I had not done anything to show I was anything but a disaster.

This turned a corner for me. I finally started to realize, at twenty-two, that I was not meant to be used and abused. My life meant something and I was created for a reason. The Creator of the Universe had a plan for my life and it was not to harm me, it was to prosper me. I can't begin to describe the hope that welled up inside me when I began to realize that I no longer had to live as a victim. I felt unstoppable. I wanted to live and not die. For the first time I knew I could do this whole "life" thing. No matter what happened I would always be okay.

Trusting the Process

Healing was a process that began with facing years of hurts, disappointments, failures, and rejection. None of the shame, guilt, and worthlessness magically went away. I had to do the work. I had to engage my failures and disappointments. Once I was able to see and admit that I was injured God was able to treat those injuries.

I needed to feel the feelings I stuffed away for so long. I had to recognize them and feel them as a vital part of my process. Just like my physical injuries, my emotional injuries had to be treated. Once I acknowledged that I needed to go through the process of healing my heart, I jumped in and the healing started. I prayed, read my bible, learned scripture, and quoted it over my life. I cried and then cried some more. I talked to people who knew more than I did. I surrounded myself with men and woman who loved me, encouraged me, answered my questions, and didn't let me settle for half healing. I shared my weaknesses with friends and asked them to help me stay away from those things.

I took the time to work through my hurts. I had to allow myself to grieve what could have been. I mourned the family and the life I thought I should have had. I needed to let those ideas go, and accept that I couldn't go back and change them. All I could do was heal and work on building the kind of life I wanted all along.

I will not lie. This process was not fun. It was absolutely gut wrenching. I spent about three months, bawling every morning, curled up under a pew during morning prayer. It felt like I was pouring rubbing alcohol over an open wound in my chest. Even through this, I knew that I had to continue to press through and fight for my victory. If I quit half way I would remain a victim and I wasn't ready to settle for that. I wanted to be a conqueror. The Bible tells us we can actually be more than conquerors.

> "In all these things, we are more than conquerors through him who loved us. For I am convinced that neither death nor life, neither angels nor demons, neither the present nor the future, nor any powers, neither height nor depth, nor anything else in all creation, will be able to separate us from the love of God that is in Christ Jesus our Lord," (Romans 8:37-39 NIV).

I no longer wanted to be defined by my mistakes and my upbringing. I was determined that I was going to change how I let my circumstances define me. I wanted my family tree of sour lemons to change into something beautiful. The only way I could do it was to become an overcomer. So, I prayed. I cried. I fought. I went to counseling. I quit some days, but I got back up the next day and kept pushing. I worshipped. I never stopped believing that God had a plan for my life. I knew he was with me and he was going to stay with me through this whole process. I reminded myself of the Word:

> "We are pressed on every side by troubles, but we are not crushed. We are perplexed, but not driven to despair. We are hunted down, but

never abandoned by God. We get knocked
down, but we are not destroyed," (2 Corinthians
4:8-10 NLT).

There were times when I thought I was healed enough. Then
there were times when the pain was so great I wanted to run
back to drugs and alcohol. I didn't want to go to God because
He wouldn't let me ignore the pain. I knew this was not an
option, so I ran to the people who would help me run to
God. They helped me feel what I needed to feel to heal the
pain. Every time I did, I came out a little happier, a little more
confident, and a little more victorious.

"Weeping may stay for the night, but rejoicing
comes in the morning," (Psalm 30:5 NIV).

I was going to get to a place of rejoicing, and I did. When I let
go of all my hurt and pain, it was freeing. I was no longer held
back by injury. God had recovered so much in me and I was
ready to conquer the world! However, I still had to allow him
to renew my mind. I had a lot of mindsets and thoughts that
were not right. I needed to learn who God said I was, how to
deal with life, and how to treat people. The Bible instructed me
to do this very thing.

"Do not conform to the pattern of this world,
but be transformed by the renewing of your

mind. Then you will be able to test and approve what God's will is—his good, pleasing and perfect will," (Romans 12:20 NIV).

Renewing my mind was a process. I had twisted and perverted views on relationships, sex, and love. Taking time to study the Bible and learn from people who had healthy views in this area was a vital part of my transformation process. I figured I needed to start renewing my mind and thought processes by focusing on the big issues I had; the promiscuity, the drugs, always being on the defense, and not trusting people. I did this by studying my Bible, learning scripture, and trying to treat people like Jesus did.

> "But you did not learn anything like this from Christ. If you have heard of Him and have learned from Him, put away the old person you used to be. Have nothing to do with your old sinful life. It was sinful because of being fooled into following bad desires. Let your minds and hearts be made new. You must become a new person and be God-like. Then you will be made right with God and have a true holy life, " (Ephesians 4:20-24 NIV).

I am still a work in progress, like everyone, but I strive to live out Ephesians 4 daily in my life.

Iron Sharpens Iron

Accountability has been vital in my success. In addition to allowing God into my broken places to bring healing and renewing my mind, I needed to be able to share my struggles with others. When I was facing disappointments or temptations it was important that a few preselected people knew. These were people I trusted and knew always had my best interests at heart. I would call them and tell them I was disappointed or having a rough day and wanted to run to old vices for comfort. They would always pray with me, remind me to turn to God for my source of comfort, and check in on me until the moment passed. My accountability partners would challenge my thinking and encourage me to dig deeper into the Word. They would always tell me what I needed to hear even if it wasn't what I wanted to hear.

> "As iron sharpens iron, so one person sharpens another," (Proverbs 27:17 NIV).

I still have accountability people in my life. They help me grow and become better, just as I do for them. We never stop needing people to walk this journey with us. In fact, the author of Hebrews encourages us not to give up meeting together:

> "Let us hold unswervingly to the hope we profess, for he who promised is faithful. And let us consider how we may spur one another

on toward love and good deeds, not giving up meeting together, as some are in the habit of doing, but encouraging one another—and all the more as you see the Day approaching," (Hebrews 10:23-25 NIV).

I encourage you to find a few people with whom you can share your dreams, successes, failures, and struggles. Make sure they are people who will pray with you through the tough struggles and failures, will challenge you when you get comfortable, encourage you to chase your dreams, and celebrate your successes with you. We all need these people in our worlds.

CHAPTER 10

EXCITED FOR THE NEXT

There Is a Future

For most of my life I questioned whether I would survive long enough to have a future. If I did have a future, I wondered if it would be filled with despair and struggle or if there might be a day when my life would be filled with hope, joy and purpose. In my late teens and twenties, I had given up on a good future, and just focused on surviving the day. When I met Jesus that all began to change. I started having more days where I woke up looking forward to the day instead of dreading it. I was excited about the life I was building and the things I was doing. There was a time, early on in my relationship with God, when I blamed him. I kept asking, *"Why did he do this to me? Why did he have to give me an abusive family and have me grow up around people who teased and bullied me? What had I done to deserve such horrible circumstances?"*

Even though I found out that God wasn't afraid of my questions or my struggles, I remember coming to a place where the whys didn't matter to me anymore. I decided in my heart that everything I went through was worth it if I could use my experiences to help change one person's life. If my story, could bring hope to even one person, and help them rise above what has been thrown at them then it was all worth it to me. I would go through it all again. My heart was beginning to be drawn to people who were in tough situations or trying to move past a painful past.

Through the process of healing I was transformed from a hard and callused girl into a strong and compassionate woman. I no longer wondered if I had a future I knew I had a one, and I was excited about it! The possibilities were endless. I still don't know all that God has in store for me, but I do know He has a plan. I want to help people be victorious, to change their family trees. People need to know that they can overcome abuse whether it's sexual, physical, or emotional. We are not defined by what other people say about us, do to us, or even by what we do to ourselves. Today is a new day.

"And they overcame him by the blood of the
Lamb and by the word of their testimony,
and they did not love their lives to the death,"
(Revelation 12:11 NKJV).

I know the more I share my story, the more I invest into others,
the more I overcome. My experiences have given me a heart
that empathizes with people.

I understand where you have been. There is a God that loves
you and wants to help you, comfort you, and guide you through
the healing process even if you don't know him yet. If you do,
just ask Him to help you. I comprehend that the process to get
up is hard. I also believe with everything in me that you can do
it. The two of you together can do anything you can imagine.

CONCLUSION

January 25, 2001 was a defining day for me. I had to choose the person I wanted to be. Was I going to be a victim or a victor? Was I going to let the hand I was dealt give me a life of despair and destruction, or was I going to fight for a better life? I was tired of surviving and decided it was time to overcome. It was my live or die moment and I chose to live. That meant I chose Jesus. He is the one that gave me the strength to fight my way out of the pit and stand on solid ground. He loved me and comforted me in a way that no one else could. That brought healing to my heart.

As my heart began to heal I knew that I didn't want anyone else to ever feel the way I felt. Although I can't control what other people feel, what I can do is share my story and experiences with others to bring hope. I have learned so much about the faithfulness and love of God. Please know that whatever you are facing, God is bigger and he will give you the strength to get through it. Just lean on him. When you are going through difficult times and it seems like everything around you, involving you, and in you is being turned upside down, just be still and know that he is God; not your situation, not your circumstances, not your hurt and pain, not your shattered dreams. God is God!! We need to find rest and peace in Him.

I want you to be encouraged and confident that you are a fighter. You are victorious. You are an overcomer. There is nothing you have done or that has been done to you to disqualify you from a relationship with God. He loves you. He wants to help you. All you have to do is let him. Trust the process because it will be a process. You can't heal gaping wounds in an instant and you won't be able to heal your heart in an instant either. I wish I could say it will be easy but I would be lying. It has taken a lot of discipline, accountability, and determination. I had to decide to allow God to be my source of comfort. I had to be vulnerable and allow people to know how I was really feeling so they could help me through the tough moments. I had to force myself to do what was right instead of what felt good in the moment.

Minute by minute and day by day I had to make choices to

no longer be defined by abuse. I had to come to a place where I was able to accept the fact that I am beautiful and adequate and worth people noticing and loving. I had to decide to love myself. I had to choose to conquer my thoughts and dismiss them daily. As I began to do this, I began to have victories I could celebrate. With each small victory, I gained a little more confidence and that motivated to keep going and to push harder. You can do this.

In 1 Samuel 17, we see the story of David and Goliath which has always fascinated me. Here was a boy who had decided that he was going to kill Goliath. Goliath had been in the army since he was a boy. It would appear that there was no way that David could kill Goliath. He didn't have the training or the weapons to kill Goliath. In this scripture, David says to Goliath:

> "You come against me with sword and spear and javelin, but I come against you in the name of the LORD Almighty, the God of the armies of Israel, whom you have defied," (1 Samuel 17:45 NIV).

What David did have was the belief that with God he could do anything. As long as God was on his side, he couldn't be defeated. We are going to face giants in our lives that in our own strength, our own ability, and our own wisdom we could never defeat. If we will pick up our God given weapons, strength, and wisdom, and trust that what God says is true, then we will be unstoppable. Don't be afraid to face your Giants. You will conquer them.

Genesis 37-45 tell the story of Joseph. Joseph was given a dream by God that he was going to rule over his family. His brothers were angered by this dream. The thought of bowing down to their little brother didn't sit well with them. They plotted to kill him but decided to throw him into a pit and sell him into slavery instead. Eventually Joseph was thrown into prison and then finally, he saw his dream come to pass. It was a twelve-year process from the time he was given the dream until it came to pass.

Joseph must have felt betrayed by his family, abandoned at times, and totally confused as to why he was in prison. The one thing Joseph never forgot was that God is faithful. Joseph had to go through the process so that his character would develop to the point that he could handle the dream. Had Joseph's dream come to pass right away, his character would not have been able to withstand what the enemy would bring against him. Often the thing that looks like an abortion of God's plan actually ends up being the road to its fulfillment, if we stay in obedience and free from offense. I want to challenge you to determine in your heart that today is the day you turn your life around. Meet God. Find a church. Read your Bible. Find and memorize scriptures that will help you in your journey. Worship. Find an accountability group. These are all practical things you can do to help you become the best you that you can be. Most importantly, NEVER, NEVER give up!

If You Don't Know God Yet

Some of you have read this book and you know God. You know who he is and what it means to have a relationship with him. Some of you have read this book and are thinking to yourself, "I want to know God. I want to have a personal relationship with Him." The great thing is you can right now.

> "If you declare with your mouth, 'Jesus is Lord,' and believe in your heart that God raised him from the dead, you will be saved. For it is with your heart thatyou believe and are justified, and it is with your mouth that you profess yourfaith and are saved," (Romans 10:9-10 NIV).

If you are reading this and you want to begin a relationship with God just say the following prayer:

Dear God,

I want to have a personal relationship with you. I confess that I don't know how. Please forgive me of my sins. I believe that Jesus was raised from the dead and I confess that he is Lord. Show yourself to me and help me know you and your will for my life. Help me Jesus, Amen.

I am so excited that you have made this decision. It is life-changing. I strongly encourage you to find a local church you can connect with to help you learn more about God, what he says about you, and develop a relationship with him.

Much love and blessings!

ABOUT THE AUTHOR

Dallas grew up in an environment filled with drugs, alcohol and abuse. After making her fair share of mistakes, she radically turned her life around through a relationship with Jesus. Her life experiences give her the ability to connect with people on a deeper level. She chooses to believe in the people no one believes in.

Dallas is a woman on a mission to help restore, encourage, and believe in broken and hurting young people through speaking and mentoring. She travels the country sharing her story, declaring truth, and sharing God's love. Her disarming vulnerability and open personality allow those around her to gain hope that through God, they too don't have to be defined by their history, present circumstances or pain.

Today, Dallas is an author, speaker and ordained minister with a Bachelors in Christian Leadership. She enjoys laughing and making people laugh, and you will usually find her in a pair of Converse™ shoes because she wears them all the time. She is a loyal, trustworthy friend and confidant whose passion is to equip people with what God says about them and help them walk out their freedom through finding their purpose.

www.dallasfreeman.com

WORKS CITED

1. New International Version. Biblica, 2011. BibleGateway.com, www.biblegateway.com/versions/New-International-Version-NIV-Bible/#booklist

2. New Living Translation. Tyndale House Publishers Inc., 2007. BibleGateway.com, www.biblegateway.com/versions/New-Living-Translation-NLT-Bible/#booklist

3. New King James Version. Thomas Nelson, 1982. BibleGateway.com, www.biblegateway.com/versions/New-King-James-Version-NKJV-Bible/#booklist

Made in the USA
Columbia, SC
25 September 2017